the TECHNOLOGY beHIND
AMAZING BUILT STRUCTURES

Nicolas Brasch

- ○ How Did the Egyptians Build the Pyramids?

- ○ Has the Statue of Liberty Always Been Green?

- ○ Whose Idea Was It to Tunnel Between Britain and France?

A⁺

Smart Apple Media
P.O. Box 3263
Mankato, MN, 56002

First published in 2010 by
MACMILLAN EDUCATION AUSTRALIA PTY LTD
15–19 Claremont St, South Yarra, Australia 3141

Visit our web site at www.macmillan.com.au or go directly to www.macmillanlibrary.com.au

Associated companies and representatives throughout the world.

Library of Congress Cataloging-in-Publication Data

Brasch, Nicolas.
    Amazing built structures / Nicolas Brasch.
        p. cm. — (The technology behind)
    Includes index.
    ISBN 978-1-59920-565-6 (library bound)
    1. Civil engineering—Juvenile literature. 2. Building—Juvenile literature. I. Title.
    TA149.B72 2011
624.1—dc22

                                                2009054432

Publisher: Carmel Heron
Managing Editor: Vanessa Lanaway
Editor: Georgina Garner
Proofreader: Erin Richards
Designer: Stella Vassiliou
Page layout: Stella Vassiliou and Raul Diche
Photo researcher: Wendy Duncan (management: Debbie Gallagher)
Illustrators: Damien Demaj, DEMAP, p. 10; Alan Laver, pp. 7, 8, 9, 12, 14, 16, 18, 20, 22, 24, 26, 27, 28, 29, 30, 31; Richard Morden, p. 23; Karen Young, p. 1 and Try This! logo.
Production Controller: Vanessa Johnson

Manufactured in China by Macmillan Production (Asia) Ltd.
Kwun Tong, Kowloon, Hong Kong
Supplier Code: CP March 2010

Acknowledgements
The author and the publisher are grateful to the following for permission to reproduce copyright material:

Front cover photographs:
Pyramids © Volker Kreinacke/iStockphoto; Eiffel Tower © Shutterstock/Andrew Buckin; Statue of Liberty © Shutterstock/Christopher Parypa.

AAP Image/AFP Photo/Antonio Scorza, **15**; Collection tour Eiffel, **16**; © Bettmann/Corbis, **18**; © Yves Forestier/Corbis, **25**; © Benjamin D. Glaha/Corbis, **21**; © Gregg Newton/Corbis, **14**; © Eurotunnel, **25**; © Alfred Eisenstaedt/Time & Life Pictures/Getty Images, **13** (bottom right); © Kaku Karita/Time & Life Pictures/Getty Images, **26**; © Maremagnum/Photographer's Choice/Getty Images, **5**; © Michel Porro/Getty Images, **30**; Guy Vandereist/Photographer's Choice/Getty Images, **31**; © Keren Su/China Span/Getty Images, **11**; © Myles Dumas/iStockphoto, **10**; © Volker Kreinacke/iStockphoto, **6**; © Mike Liu/iStockphoto, **23**; © Lambert (Bart) Parren/iStockphoto, **8**; © Chris Schmidt/iStockphoto, **4**; photolibrary/Science Photo Library, **24** (bottom); © Shutterstock/Andrew Buckin, **17**; © Shutterstock/Patrik Dietrich, **28** (right); © Shutterstock/Rich Koele, **12**; © Shutterstock/Christopher Parypa, **19**; U.S. Bureau of Reclamation, **20**; US National Park Service, **13** (top right, bottom left).

While every care has been taken to trace and acknowledge copyright, the publisher tenders their apologies for any accidental infringement where copyright has proved untraceable. Where the attempt has been unsuccessful, the publisher welcomes information that would redress the situation.

The publisher would like to thank Heidi Ruhnau, Head of Science at Oxley College, for her assistance in reviewing manuscripts.

Please note
At the time of printing, the Internet addresses appearing in this book were correct. Owing to the dynamic nature of the Internet, however, we cannot guarantee that all these addresses will remain correct.

▶ Contents

Word Watch

Web Watch

Look out for these features throughout the book:

"Word Watch" explains the meanings of words shown in **bold**

"Web Watch" provides web site suggestions for further research

What Is Technology?

The First Tools
One of the first examples of technology, where humans used their knowledge of the world to their advantage, was when humans began shaping and carving stone and metals into tools such as axes and chisels.

▲ People use technology every day, such as when they turn on computers. Technology is science put into action to help humans and solve problems.

Technology is the use of **science** for practical purposes, such as building bridges, inventing machines, and improving materials. Humans have been using technology since they built the first shelters and lit the first fires.

Technology in People's Lives

Technology is behind many things in people's everyday lives, from lightbulbs to can openers. It has shaped the sports shoes people wear and helped them run faster. Cars, trains, airplanes, and space shuttles are all products of technology. Engineers use technology to design and construct materials and structures such as bridges, roads, and buildings. Technology can be seen in amazing built structures all around humans.

Technology is responsible for how people communicate with each other. Information technology uses scientific knowledge to determine ways to spread information widely and quickly. Recently, this has involved the creation of the Internet, and e-mail and file-sharing technologies. In the future, technology may become even more a part of people's lives, with the development of robots and artificial intelligence for use in business, in the home, and in science.

The Technology Behind Amazing Built Structures

From the moment humans began to build shelters, they have been using technology to create built structures. Humans have also become fascinated with building the biggest, longest, largest, heaviest, and most amazing structures they can.

Practical and Inspiring Structures

Many things drive people to build structures that test limits such as height and length. Often, the structures they create have specific and practical purposes, such as housing people, bridging rivers, or linking two countries by road. Skyscrapers are designed to house a large number of people and businesses in small spaces, which is why the first skyscrapers were built in crowded cities, such as Chicago and New York. The Egyptian pyramids were built for a specific purpose, too, as tombs for the **pharaohs**. Stonehenge and the Great Wall of China are other examples of ancient structures that were built for specific reasons.

Sometimes, the structures that people build are **monuments** or pieces of art. The Statue of Liberty, Christ the Redeemer, and the Eiffel Tower may not have obvious practical purposes, but they are amazing demonstrations of technology and human achievement.

The People Behind the Technology

Many people with different jobs are behind the technology of amazing structures.

Architect Designing a building or other structure

Structural Engineer Planning, designing, and supervising the construction of bridges, buildings, and other structures

Riveter Putting **rivets** into structures, such as bridges

▲ Some built structures, such as the Statue of Liberty in New York, are inspirational.

Word Watch

monuments buildings or other structures that are built to honor someone or something

pharaohs ancient Egyptian kings

rivets metal pins used for holding pieces of metal together

How Did the Egyptians Build the Pyramids?

From around 2630 B.C. to 1600 B.C., the ancient Egyptians built large triangular structures, called pyramids, as tombs and **monuments** to their **pharaohs**. Archaeologists, historians, and scientists have worked out many details of how these pyramids were built, but some mysteries still remain.

▲ The pyramids at Giza were originally covered in smooth stone, but most of this outer layer has been destroyed. Like other Egyptian pyramids, the Giza pyramids are made up of enormous stone slabs.

Disagreement

Some archaeologists disagree with the theory that the Egyptians flooded the ground to help them get the base level. They argue that the temperature in Egypt is so hot that too much water would have evaporated for this to work.

Plotting the Base

Egyptian pyramids have a base with four sides. The Egyptians always arranged the four sides so that two ran in a north–south direction and two ran east–west. Compasses had not been invented yet, but it is thought that the Egyptians found correct directions by placing poles in the ground to mark the shadow of the sun at certain times of the day.

Leveling the Ground

Before construction could begin, the ground had to be made level. One **theory** about how this was done is that the Egyptians cut **trenches** into the limestone that was below the surface sand and then flooded the site with water. The water in the trenches would sit level. The workers would then cut away all the visible stone until they reached this level waterline.

Cutting the Stone

The pyramids were made from various types of stone. Limestone was very popular, and most of it came from a **quarry** only 1,000 feet (300 m) from where the Great Pyramid was built at Giza. In the quarry, the sand and rubble above the limestone were removed, and workers used copper and stone tools to cut slabs of rock. Long wooden levers were then forced under each slab, and the slab was lifted up. Ropes were tied around the slab, and the slab was placed on a **sledge**.

Transporting the Stone

If the stone slabs came from a quarry near the pyramid site, workers pulled the sledge along specially constructed roadways to the site. Some highly prized stones needed to be transported hundreds of miles, so these stones were transported by boat along the Nile River.

Construction

The main problem facing both the designers and builders of the pyramids was how to set the stones as the pyramid got higher. Archaeologists believe the Egyptians used a ramp system, but they disagree on the sort of ramp used.

pyramid

ramp

▲ During construction, the Egyptians may have used a spiral ramp, which wrapped its way around the pyramid.

pyramid

ramp

▲ A zigzag ramp, built on one side of the pyramid, may have been used to construct the pyramids.

pyramid

ramp

▶ A long, straight ramp, built on one side of the pyramid, may have been used during construction.

Heavy Stone Slabs
The Great Pyramid of Giza was made from more than 2 million slabs of stone. The average weight of these slabs was 5,500 pounds (2,500 kg).

Pyramid Workers
Some people think that the Egyptians used slaves to build the pyramids, but only some workers were slaves. Most workers were either paid for their work or carried out the work as a form of taxation to the pharaoh.

Word Watch

quarry place where stone or other materials are dug up

sledge cart with runners that slide across the ground, used to transport goods and people

Web Watch ▼

www.touregypt.net/ construction

www.catchpenny.org/ howbuilt.html

What Is Stonehenge and Who Built It?

Stonehenge is a stone **henge** in England. This mysterious **monument** was built by the ancient people of Britain over a period of almost 2,000 years. There are several **theories** as to what Stonehenge was used for and how it was built.

▲ Stonehenge is in Wiltshire, southern England.

▲ Stonehenge is a prehistoric structure, which means it was built before written records.

What Might Stonehenge Be?

It is thought that Stonehenge might have been used as an altar, where animals or even humans were sacrificed to the gods, or as a place to observe the skies and calculate when solar and lunar **eclipses** would occur. A recent theory is that people came to Stonehenge to be healed. Its bluestones were thought to have healing powers.

How Stonehenge Was Built

Stonehenge was built in three stages between 3100 B.C. and about 1600 B.C.

1 » The first stage of building was between 3100 B.C. and 2900 B.C. A circular **bank** was constructed at the Stonehenge site. A ditch was dug outside the bank, and 56 holes were dug inside the bank. These holes are now known as the Aubrey holes. The holes may have been used to support wooden posts. The digging was done by hand, probably using animal bones and deer antlers.

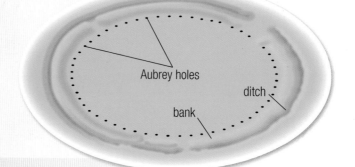

Aubrey holes

ditch

bank

2 ›› About 2300 B.C., large bluestone pillars, weighing about 4.4 tons, (4 t) each, were erected at the center of the circle. Amazingly, these huge slabs of stone came from the Preseli Mountains in Wales, 150 miles (240 km) from Stonehenge.

There are two main theories as to how these slabs were brought from the Preseli Mountains to Stonehenge. Some historians believe the slabs were transported by land and sea on rollers, **sledges**, and rafts. A more recent theory suggests they may have been carried by a **glacier** before they settled near the Stonehenge site.

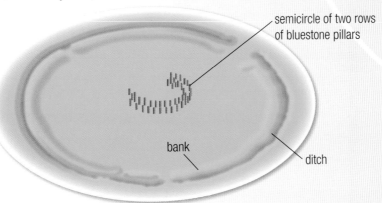

semicircle of two rows of bluestone pillars

bank

ditch

3 ›› The third stage of construction started about 2000 B.C. Even longer and heavier stone slabs, known as the Sarsen stones, were transported to the site and erected. These slabs came from the Marlborough Downs, about 19 miles (30 km) from Stonehenge. Some weighed up to 55 ton (50 t) and were transported using ropes and sledges. Modern **reenactments** and calculations suggest that it took at least 500 men to pull each stone.

Blocks of stone, called lintels, lay horizontally atop the slabs. Each lintel block was shaped to the curve of the circle and fitted end-to-end, using **tongue-and-groove joints**. They were attached using **ball-and-socket joints**. This reflected the technology of the time.

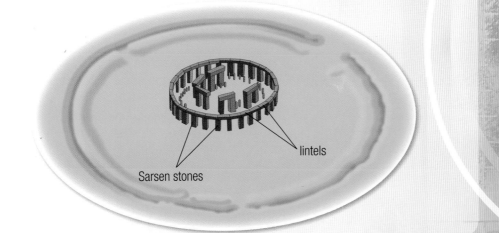

lintels

Sarsen stones

Aubrey Holes
The Aubrey holes are so named because some of them were thought to have been discovered by the writer John Aubrey in 1666.

Word Watch

ball-and-socket joints joining areas where a round ball sits in a socket, allowing movement in many directions

glacier huge mass of ice that slowly moves over land

reenactments recreations of events, as close as possible to how they originally occurred

sledges carts with runners that slide across the ground, used to transport goods and people

tongue-and-groove joints joining areas where two planks are joined by interlocking ridges and grooves

What Is the Longest Wall in the World?

The Great Wall of China is the longest wall in the world! It is sometimes said that the Great Wall of China can be seen from space with the naked eye, but no human-made structure can be seen from space without a telescope or other instrument.

Origin of the Wall

The Great Wall of China is not a single wall but many different walls that were built over more than 2,000 years. The first walls were built around 475 B.C. to 221 B.C., during a period known as the Warring States Period. During this time, China was not a united country but consisted of many different states, all with their own rulers. Many of these states built walls to protect themselves from each other. The oldest part of the Great Wall is believed to have been built by the Qi state.

World Heritage Site

In 1987, the Great Wall of China was proclaimed a United Nations Educational, Scientific and Cultural Organization (UNESCO) World Heritage Site. It is valued for a number of reasons, including because it represents "a masterpiece of human creative genius."

Web Watch

www.greatwall-of-china.com/
whc.unesco.org/en/list/438
www.travelchinaguide.com/
china_great_wall/scene/

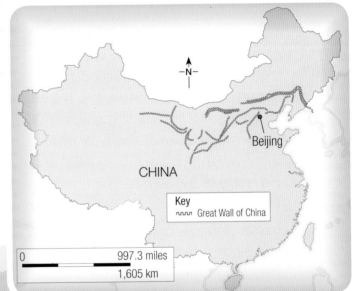

▶ The Great Wall of China stretches across northeastern China for more than 2,100 miles (3,400 km), with many more thousands of miles of wall branching off of the main wall.

CHINA

Beijing

-N-

Key
~~~ Great Wall of China

0   997.3 miles
           1,605 km

◀ The towers along the Great Wall were used as viewing points and attack posts.

Qin Dynasty

In 221 B.C., Qin Shi Huang conquered all the states and created a united China under his rule. The period from 221 B.C. to 206 B.C. is known as the Qin Dynasty.

Although Qin did not feel threatened by those he had conquered, he did fear an invasion from the Xiongnu people in northern China. To protect his land, Qin ordered that the gaps between all the existing walls be filled with new walls and that the whole wall be extended to cover thousands of miles. The new sections were made by mixing pounded earth with **gravel**. This mixture was supported by wooden frames.

▶ Under Qin Shi Huang, many pieces of wall were joined to create the Great Wall of China. Very little of this stone and wood wall remains today. This statue was built in Qin's honor.

Height and Width

The Great Wall is up to 26 feet (8 m) high and 18 feet (5.5 m) wide. The width was designed to allow for soldiers to march in groups of up to 10 people across, along the top of the wall.

Bones in the Wall?

According to Chinese legend, the bones of the workers who died while building the wall during the Qin Dynasty were used to build the wall, too.

Ming Dynasty

Many emperors ruled after Qin repaired and added to the wall, but no major changes were made until the Ming Dynasty (1368–1644). Under the various emperors of this period, the wall was rebuilt and extended, particularly along the northern border of the country and around the capital, Beijing. This was to stop invasions from Mongolia and Manchuria in the north.

Most of the wall that stands today was built during the Ming Dynasty. These parts of the wall were much stronger than previous walls. They were constructed using stone and bricks and had towers built along them.

Word Watch

gravel mixture of stones and sand

Who Carved Four U.S. Presidents into a Mountain?

Mount Rushmore National Memorial is a sculpture of the heads of four U.S. presidents, carved into a mountain in South Dakota. It was carved by several hundred workers under the guidance of sculptor Gutzon Borglum between 1927 and 1941.

Sunlit Sculpture

Gutzon Borglum chose Mount Rushmore because if was thick enough to support the carvings and it captured more sunlight than surrounding mountains.

▶ Mount Rushmore National Memorial is located near Keystone, South Dakota.

◀ Mount Rushmore National Memorial features the faces of U.S. Presidents George Washington, Thomas Jefferson, Theodore Roosevelt, and Abraham Lincoln.

The Idea for the Sculpture

The original idea for a massive carving in South Dakota came from a local historian, Doane Robinson. He wanted to attract tourists to South Dakota and raise the state's profile. He contacted the well-known sculptor Gutzon Borglum in 1924, and Borglum was very keen to be involved.

Robinson wanted the carvings to represent local identities but Borglum was more interested in featuring national identities. Borglum also rejected Robinson's preferred location and selected Mount Rushmore instead. Eventually, the two men agreed to feature the faces of four U.S. presidents—George Washington, Thomas Jefferson, Abraham Lincoln, and Theodore Roosevelt—making the sculpture a celebration of the first 150 years of modern U.S. history.

Carving the Mountain

The first stage of the Mount Rushmore project involved Gutzon Borglum making a model of the sculpture in his studio.

Before work could begin on the mountain, a stairway to the top was constructed. Cables were fixed along the path of the stairway. Borglum's workers fixed harnesses to these cables so they could be safely suspended while they worked.

The surface rock of the mountain was blasted with dynamite. The workers started drilling holes to form a honeycomb pattern, then they slowly chipped away at the stone to form the required shapes and angles. The drills that the workers used weighed almost 90 pounds (40 kg).

▲ A worker prepares dynamite for blasting the rock. One of Borglum's models hangs behind him.

▲ The workers chipped away at the rock piece by piece.

◄ The eyes of the presidents are massive holes, but a **granite** cube was left in each eye to represent the pupil. The position of these cubes means that sunlight catches them and the eyes look more realistic.

The Presidents

- George Washington was the first president of the United States, from 1789 to 1797. He had previously led Americans in their battle for independence against the British.
- Thomas Jefferson was the third president, from 1801 to 1809. He was also an inventor and philosopher.
- Abraham Lincoln was the sixteenth president, from 1861 to 1865. He led the country when it was engaged in the American Civil War (1861–65) and **oversaw** the end of slavery.
- Theodore Roosevelt was the twenty-sixth president, from 1901 to 1909. He is considered one of the fairest presidents, because he did not favor either business or workers over each other.

Word Watch

granite very hard rock made up of quartz and other stones

oversaw supervised or watched over

Web Watch ▼

www.nps.gov/moru

13

What Is the Christ the Redeemer Statue Made From?

Christ the Redeemer is a 125-foot (38-m) high statue that overlooks the city of Rio de Janeiro in Brazil. Most of the statue is made from concrete, but the outside is coated with soapstone, a type of rock that is **resistant** to sun, wind, and rain.

Cristo Redentor

Christ the Redeemer is another name for Jesus Christ, the central person in the Christian religion. In Brazil's national language, Portuguese, the statue is known as Cristo Redentor.

Brazil

SOUTH AMERICA

Rio de Janeiro
Corcovado

—N—

0   621 miles
   1,000 km

98 feet (30 m) wide, from fingertip to fingertip

125 feet (38 m) tall, including **pedestal**

▲ The Christ the Redeemer statue stands on top of Corcovado, a mountain beside Rio de Janeiro in Brazil.

▲ Christ the Redeemer is a stone statue weighing 1,262 tons (1,145 t)—which is 2,524,000 pounds (1,145,000 kg)!

From Idea to Design

As far back as the mid-1800s, the idea of constructing a statue on top of Corcovado was discussed. Brazil is a very Catholic country, and various religious proposals were suggested. When the country became a **republic** in 1889, however, laws were passed to keep the government and churches separate, so government money could not be spent on a religious **monument**.

In 1921, leaders of the Catholic Church in Brazil began to organize the building of a massive statue of Jesus Christ on top of Corcovado Mountain. They ran a competition to find the best design and raised money to pay for the costs of designing and building the statue. The designer was Brazilian engineer Heitor da Silva Costa, while the sculptor was Frenchman Paul Landowski.

Constructing the Statue

Several models of the statue were built, and various calculations were carried out before the final version was selected. Soapstone was chosen for most of the outside of the statue, because it lasts a long time and is easier to carve than other stones.

The construction was **overseen** by da Silva Costa. Construction was made difficult because of the site's location at the top of a mountain, but the materials and workers were carried up to the site by train.

First, the main structure of the statue was built using reinforced concrete. Reinforced concrete has **steel** bars or wire mesh within the concrete, making the structure stronger. Finally, parts such as the head and hands were added.

After nine years of fund-raising and building, Christ the Redeemer was officially unveiled on October 12, 1931.

Soapstone Protection

In February 2008, an electrical storm hit Rio de Janeiro and lightning strikes destroyed buildings and other structures. Christ the Redeemer was not damaged because soapstone acts as an **insulator**.

Word Watch

insulator material that is able to resist an electrical current

overseen supervised or watched over

steel strong material that is a combination of iron and carbon

▲ Two workers wash the face of Christ the Redeemer in 2000.

Christ the Redeemer Today

The train up the mountain still operates today, taking tourists from the bottom of the mountain to the site of the statue in 17 minutes. Once at the site, visitors still have to climb more than 200 steps to the foot of the statue—or they can take an escalator or elevator.

Web Watch

www.corcovado.com.br
www.copacabana.info/christ-the-redeemer.html

Why Was the Eiffel Tower Built?

Built for the World's Fair in Paris, France, in 1889, the Eiffel Tower was designed as a **monument** to modern technology. At the time, iron was used in the construction of bridges and other **infrastructure**, but it was not seen as a visually exciting material. Gustave Eiffel and his tower changed that.

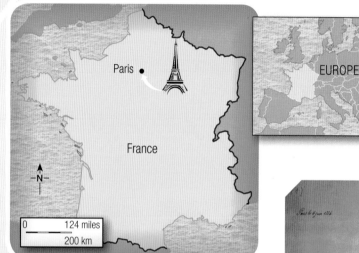

▲ The Eiffel Tower is located in Paris, France.

Designing the Tower

Plans were made for an iron tower to serve as a landmark for the 1899 World's Fair. More than 100 drawings and plans were submitted. Judges determined that the design by Gustave Eiffel was the best entry. Eiffel wanted to build the tallest human-made structure in the world in the center of Paris and he wanted to build it out of **wrought iron**. Iron is very structurally useful, but Eiffel wanted to prove that iron could be visually appealing, too.

More than 5,000 design drawings were produced before construction began. The tower had to be designed to **resist** strong winds.

▲ Design plans were made by the engineers on the project, Maurice Koechlin and Emile Nouguier.

Building the Tower

The Eiffel Tower was built like a toy building from a construction kit. More than 18,000 pieces were built in a factory on the edge of Paris. The pieces were then transported to the site and assembled by more than 100 workers. The workers used wooden scaffolding and small cranes to put the pieces together.

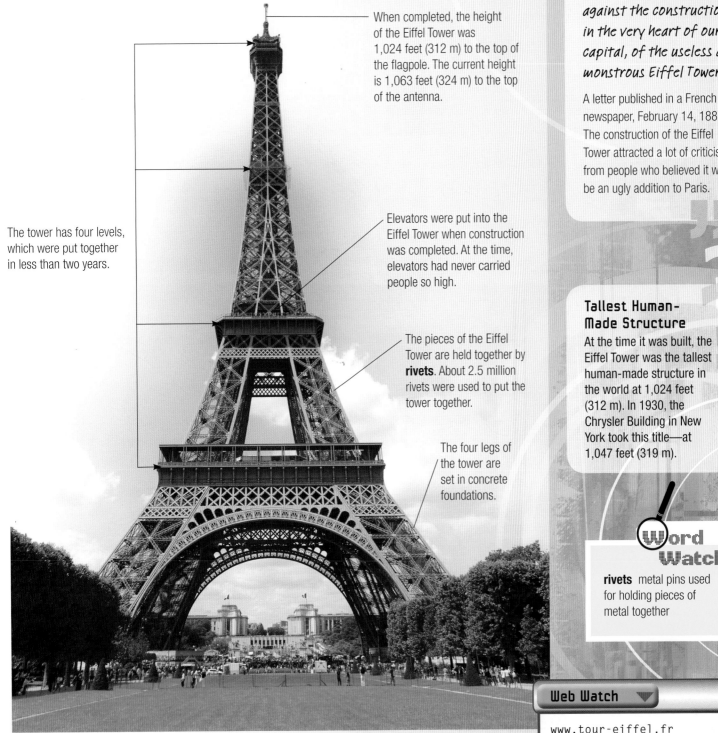

When completed, the height of the Eiffel Tower was 1,024 feet (312 m) to the top of the flagpole. The current height is 1,063 feet (324 m) to the top of the antenna.

The tower has four levels, which were put together in less than two years.

Elevators were put into the Eiffel Tower when construction was completed. At the time, elevators had never carried people so high.

The pieces of the Eiffel Tower are held together by **rivets**. About 2.5 million rivets were used to put the tower together.

The four legs of the tower are set in concrete foundations.

▲ The Eiffel Tower was to have been torn down after 20 years, but it was kept and used as a radio and television transmission tower.

We, writers, painters, sculptors, architects, passionate lovers of the beauty, until now intact, of Paris, hereby protest with all our might ... in the name of French taste gone unrecognized, in the name of French art and history under threat, against the construction, in the very heart of our capital, of the useless and monstrous Eiffel Tower.

A letter published in a French newspaper, February 14, 1887. The construction of the Eiffel Tower attracted a lot of criticism from people who believed it would be an ugly addition to Paris.

Tallest Human-Made Structure

At the time it was built, the Eiffel Tower was the tallest human-made structure in the world at 1,024 feet (312 m). In 1930, the Chrysler Building in New York took this title—at 1,047 feet (319 m).

Word Watch

rivets metal pins used for holding pieces of metal together

Web Watch ▼

www.tour-eiffel.fr

Has the Statue of Liberty Always Been Green?

The Statue of Liberty in New York represents a woman holding a torch in her right hand and a book of laws in her left. This 305-foot (93-m) high symbol of **liberty** and **enlightenment** has a **steel** skeleton and a thin copper surface. Over time, the copper surface has turned grayish green.

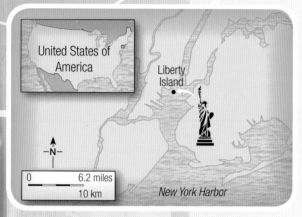

▲ The Statue of Liberty stands on Liberty Island at the entrance to New York Harbor.

▲ Bartholdi (second from right) watches over the construction of the steel frame of the statue's left hand.

Designing the Statue

The Statue of Liberty was designed and built in France and transported to the United States. It was a gift from the French people to mark 100 years of American independence in 1876, but it was not finished until 1886.

The statue was designed by French sculptor Frédéric-Auguste Bartholdi. He was helped by engineers Gustave Eiffel and Maurice Koechlin, who designed the Eiffel Tower (see pages 16–17). Their job was to design a steel skeleton frame onto which sheets of copper would be attached. The frame needed to hold the weight of the copper and remain stable. Building the statue was the responsibility of the French, but the Americans built the stone **pedestal**.

Transporting the Statue

The Statue of Liberty traveled to America on a French ship, *Isère*, in 350 pieces packed into 214 crates. It arrived in June 1885. Once the pedestal was completed in April 1886, it took four months for the statue to be reassembled. The official **dedication** of the Statue of Liberty took place on October 28, 1886.

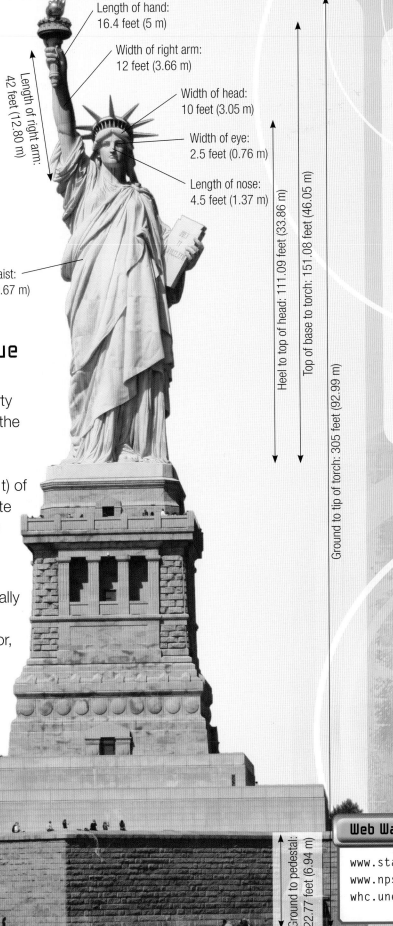

Length of hand:
16.4 feet (5 m)

Width of right arm:
12 feet (3.66 m)

Width of head:
10 feet (3.05 m)

Width of eye:
2.5 feet (0.76 m)

Length of nose:
4.5 feet (1.37 m)

Length of right arm:
42 feet (12.80 m)

Width of waist:
35 feet (10.67 m)

Heel to top of head: 111.09 feet (33.86 m)

Top of base to torch: 151.08 feet (46.05 m)

Ground to tip of torch: 305 feet (92.99 m)

Ground to pedestal:
22.77 feet (6.94 m)

▶ The full name of the statue is the Statue of Liberty Enlightening the World.

Building the Statue

The weight of the copper used in the Statue of Liberty is 31 tons (28 t), although the copper sheeting is only 0.1 inch (2.37 mm) thick. There were 125 tons (113 t) of steel used and the concrete foundation weighs 27,000 tons (24,500 t).

The Statue of Liberty's copper surface was originally a reddish brown color. Its modern greyish green color, called a patina, has been caused by **oxidation**.

> Give me your tired, your poor,
> Your huddled masses yearning to breathe free,
> The wretched refuse of your teeming shore.
> Send these, the homeless, tempest-tost to me,
> I lift my lamp beside the golden door!

Part of a poem by Emma Lazarus, carved on the base of the Statue of Liberty. The statue has welcomed many immigrants as they sailed into New York.

Word Watch

oxidation chemical reaction that occurs when some metals, such as copper, are combined with oxygen

Web Watch

www.statueofliberty.org
www.nps.gov/stli
whc.unesco.org/en/list/307

How Was the Hoover Dam Built?

The Hoover Dam was built between 1931 and 1936, providing many Americans with much needed jobs. More than 105 million cubic feet (3 million cubic meters) of concrete were used to construct the dam and nearby structures.

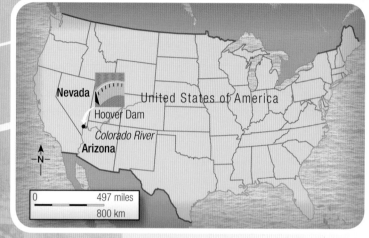

▲ The Hoover Dam is located on the Colorado River between Arizona and Nevada.

Herbert Hoover

The Hoover Dam was named after Herbert Hoover, who oversaw the planning of the dam as Secretary of Commerce. He was President of the United States when construction began.

Providing Jobs

The land surrounding the Hoover Dam is among the hottest and driest in the United States. The dam was built to provide water to **irrigate** the land for farming. It was also built to generate electricity.

At the time the dam was built, the United States was suffering because of the **Great Depression**. Jobs were hard to find, so thousands of workers flocked to the Nevada–Arizona border to work on the Hoover Dam project. A town was built to house thousands of workers, their families, and the government officials who were **overseeing** the dam's construction. The town was named Boulder City.

▼ Thousands of workers traveled to Boulder City to build the dam. These workers dug diversion tunnels through the rocky ground.

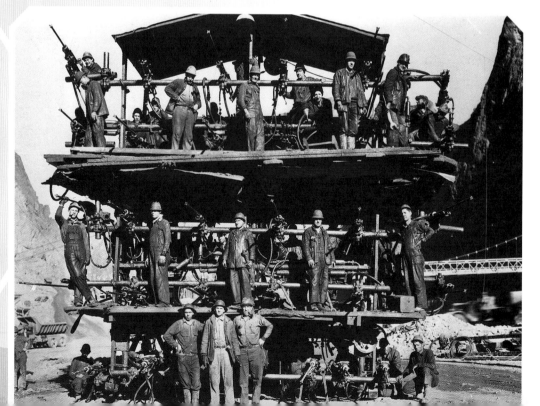

Constructing the Hoover Dam

Before construction work began, tunnels were dug to **divert** water from the Colorado River away from the site of the dam.

Creating the Base

Once the water was diverted, the bottom of the river had to be **excavated** to create the base of the dam. Mud, rock, and other materials were removed. More than 148,300,000 cubic feet (4,200,000 cu m) of materials were excavated in the construction of the dam and the diversion tunnels.

Creating the Concrete Dam

Once the base had been created, the massive job of pouring concrete began. It was calculated that if all the concrete was poured at once, it would take 125 years for it to cool to the required temperature to harden. Instead, the dam was built as a series of interlocking concrete columns.

Six Companies Inc.

The job of constructing the Hoover Dam was so big that no one company could build the dam on its own. Six large companies combined to build the dam, calling themselves Six Companies Inc.

Word Watch

divert cause something to change course or direction
excavated dug up and removed

columns of concrete layers

▲ The concrete dam was built in columns. The concrete for each column was poured in layers and each layer was no more than 6 inches (15 cm) thick. Cold water was piped through to chill the concrete, too.

Web Watch

www.usbr.gov/lc/hooverdam
www.hooverdamtourcompany.com

Why Does the Gateway Arch Sway in the Wind?

Due to its height and shape, the Gateway Arch in Missouri sways in the wind. In slight winds, it sways about half an inch (1.25 cm), but it has been designed to sway a maximum of 17.7 inches (45 cm) in winds of 145 miles (230 km) per hour.

◀ The Gateway Arch is located on the banks of the Mississippi River in St. Louis, Missouri.

The Curve Of a Chain

In the 1600s, Dutch mathematician Christiaan Huygens named the catenary curve from the Latin word *catenarius*, which means "related to a chain."

Web Watch ▼

www.gatewayarch. com
www.nps.gov/jeff/

Designing the Arch

The Gateway Arch was designed by Eero Saarinen, an architect who was born in Finland but grew up in the United States. The arch is shaped like an upside-down catenary curve. A catenary curve is the shape that a chain makes when held loosely with both ends at the same level. An upside-down catenary curve is a very strong, stable structure that is often used to build bridges, domes, and arches. The Gateway Arch was designed to withstand strong winds and earthquakes by swaying with the movement.

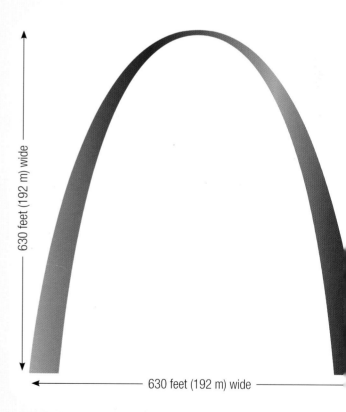

630 feet (192 m) wide

630 feet (192 m) wide

▲ The height of the Gateway Arch is the same as the distance between its two legs on the ground.

Building the Arch

The Gateway Arch was built between 1963 and 1965. It is made from **steel** and concrete. Almost 5,512 tons (5,000 t) of steel and 41,900 tons (38,000 t) of concrete were used.

The two legs of the arch were built at the same time. This meant that the mathematical formula that the arch was designed around had to be perfect, otherwise the two sides of the arch would not meet in the middle. The foundations of the two legs were sunk 59 feet (18 m) into the ground.

The interior of the arch is hollow. A tram system runs through the inside, taking visitors from the base to an observation deck at the top of the arch.

▲ The Gateway Arch forms part of the St. Louis skyline.

Try This! Creating Catenary Curves

Ask a friend to hold on to a 5 feet (1.5 m) piece of rope, wire, or chain, with one end in each hand. Tell your friend to hold her arms straight out in front of her. The curve shape that you see is a catenary curve.

Take another piece that is about 2.5 feet (75 cm) long. Again, ask your friend to hold this out in front of her, but ask her to move her arms further apart. The curve is very different from the first shape, but this is a catenary curve too.

5 feet (1.5 m)

Word Watch

monument building or other structure that is built to honor someone or something

steel strong material that is a combination of iron and carbon

Whose Idea Was It to Tunnel Between Britain and France?

The Channel Tunnel runs underneath the sea between Britain and France. The tunnel was built between 1987 and 1994, but plans for a tunnel date back to 1802—well before cars and trains even existed.

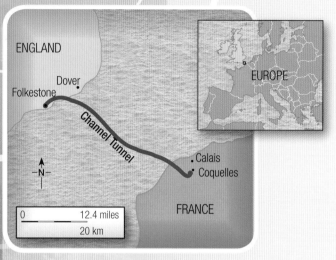

▲ The Channel Tunnel links Folkestone in southern England with Coquelles in northern France.

Mathieu's Proposal

The first proposal for a tunnel linking England and France came in 1802 from a French engineer, Albert Mathieu. He suggested the idea to Napoleon Bonaparte, the military leader who later proclaimed himself emperor of France. However, a tunnel would only work if Britain and France agreed, and by 1804 the two countries were at war and plans for a tunnel were not revived for many years.

De Gamond's Proposal

In the 1850s, Frenchman Aimé Thomé de Gamond came up with a plan that involved creating a rail tunnel that passed through an artificial island between the two countries. He even dived to the bottom of the sea to determine the **composition** of the seabed. Nothing came of his proposal.

▼ Mathieu's idea for a tunnel under the channel included airshafts so that horses and passengers could breathe.

Naming the Tunnel
In English, the Channel Tunnel is sometimes called the Chunnel. In French, it is called *Le tunnel sous le Manche* (the tunnel under the sea).

Surveying the Seabed

In the 1870s, relations between Britain and France had improved enough for the two countries to start cooperating again. They **financed** the first thorough **survey** of the seabed. Some samples were collected at sea using steamships and other samples were collected on land by digging deep shafts.

Digging Begins—and Then Stops

In the early 1880s, the digging of a cross-channel tunnel began. Workers dug a couple of miles from both France and England. The British, however, got suspicious of the French Government's **motive** for the tunnel, believing it could be used to launch an invasion. They withdrew their permission for the tunnel to go ahead.

Finally, the Tunnel Is Built

Agreement was reached again in 1973, and construction began in December 1987. The Channel Tunnel was officially opened on May 6, 1994.

There are actually three tunnels, two of which are used for train services and the other for maintenance purposes. The tunnels are 31 miles (50 km) long, with 23.6 miles (38 km) of tunnel running under the sea.

Tunnel Needed
The failure to build the tunnel in the 1880s proved costly later. During World War I (1914–18), when Germany invaded France, British soldiers could have reached mainland Europe and helped France much more quickly if there had been a tunnel.

Word Watch

financed provided money for

motive reason for doing something

survey examination and recording of the features of an area

◀ Two railway tracks lead into the Channel Tunnel entrance in the countryside of coastal France. The Channel Tunnel is used by the Eurostar passenger train, freight trains carrying goods, and the Eurotunnel Shuttle train, which carries cars and trucks.

Web Watch ▼

www.eurotunnel.com

Can the Akashi–Kaikyo Bridge Withstand an Earthquake?

Japan is located along the Ring of Fire, an area around the Pacific Ocean that experiences many earthquakes. Because of this, the Akashi–Kaikyo Bridge in Japan was built to withstand extreme earthquakes. It was also built to withstand extreme winds.

Longest and Tallest Suspension Bridge

The Akashi–Kaikyo Bridge is the world's longest and tallest suspension bridge. A suspension bridge is a bridge where the weight of the **deck** is supported by cables that are suspended from tower structures.

The central **span** of the bridge is 6,532 feet (1,991 m) long. Taking into account the other two spans and the approaches on each side, the total length of the bridge is 12,831 feet (3,911 m). The Akashi–Kaikyo Bridge also has taller towers than any other bridge in the world. They stand 1,125 feet (343 m) tall, including the foundations.

▶ The Akashi–Kaikyo Bridge is located in Japan, in an area of extreme volcanic and earthquake activity called the Ring of Fire.

▼ The Akashi–Kaikyo Bridge crosses the Akashi Strait, linking the city of Kobe, on the island of Honshū, with Iwaya, on Awaji Island. It is also known as the Pearl Bridge.

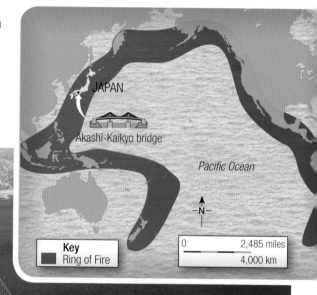

JAPAN

Akashi-Kaikyo bridge

Pacific Ocean

—N—

Key	
	Ring of Fire

0	2,485 miles
	4,000 km

Word Watch

deck the roadway or walkway of a bridge

span arch or part of a bridge between supports

Withstanding Earthquakes and Wind

The Akashi–Kaikyo Bridge has several features that protect it from extreme natural elements.

Earthquake Effects

The Akashi–Kaikyo Bridge was meant to be shorter than it is today. An extreme earthquake in 1995, known as the Kobe earthquake, shifted the towers 3.28 feet (1 m) apart while the bridge was being built, so the bridge had to be built 3.28 feet (1 m) longer.

Beneath the deck and roadway is a **network** of **trusses**, which are triangular **braces**. This strengthens the bridge so that it is able to withstand earthquakes, and it also allows strong gusts of wind to flow through the bridge.

Inside the towers are **mechanical** weights called tuned mass dampers. These weights swing the opposite way to strong winds, balancing the bridge.

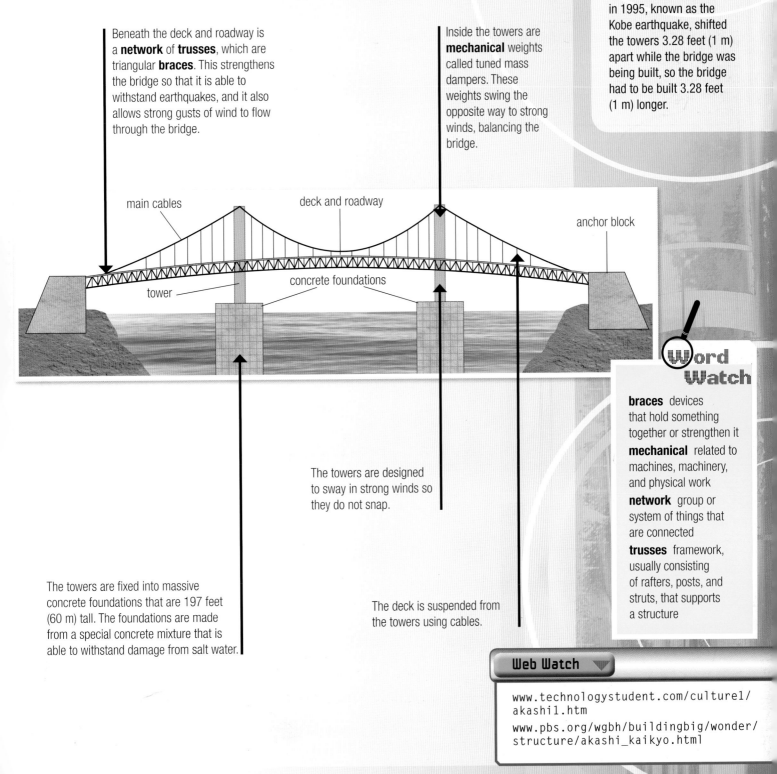

main cables

deck and roadway

anchor block

tower

concrete foundations

The towers are designed to sway in strong winds so they do not snap.

The towers are fixed into massive concrete foundations that are 197 feet (60 m) tall. The foundations are made from a special concrete mixture that is able to withstand damage from salt water.

The deck is suspended from the towers using cables.

Word Watch

braces devices that hold something together or strengthen it

mechanical related to machines, machinery, and physical work

network group or system of things that are connected

trusses framework, usually consisting of rafters, posts, and struts, that supports a structure

Web Watch ▼

www.technologystudent.com/culture1/akashi1.htm

www.pbs.org/wgbh/buildingbig/wonder/structure/akashi_kaikyo.html

Which Is the Tallest Building in the World?

At different times, the CN Tower, the Empire State Building, and Petronas Towers have been the tallest building in the world. Today, however, the tallest building is Burj Khalifa in Dubai. On January 17, 2009, it reached the height of 2,684 feet (818 m).

Designing Burj Khalifa

One of the main inspirations for the design of Burj Khalifa was the *Hymenocallis* flower, which grows in Dubai. The architect, Adrian Smith, was also inspired by the surrounding desert and its light, as well as by traditional Islamic architecture.

◀ Burj Khalifa is in Dubai in the United Arab Emirates.

◀ Burj Khalifa towers over other skyscrapers in Dubai.

Constructing Burj Khalifa

Construction of the Burj Khalifa began on September 21, 2004. Most of the building was constructed using reinforced concrete and **steel**. Concrete had to be poured in the evening and at night when temperatures were cooler. If the concrete had been poured during the heat of the Dubai day, it might have cracked.

One important feature is the shape of the building. The shape changes at various points so that the wind reacts differently at different parts of the building. This stops the wind hitting the building as one strong force.

Word Watch

steel strong material that is a combination of iron and carbon

Web Watch

www.burjkhalifa.ae
www.burjdubaisky
scraper.com

History of Skyscrapers

Skyscrapers are very tall buildings with many storeys. The first skyscraper was built in Chicago in 1885. It was 10 storeys high.

Around the same time, other skyscrapers began to be built, particularly in the United States. One of the main reasons that skyscrapers were not built before this was that designers and builders did not have the right materials and technology to ensure that the structures would stay up. The pressure on skyscrapers, from their own weight and from the wind, is enormous. By the late 1800s, however, designers and engineers had realized that a strong steel structure would hold the weight of the concrete required to construct a skyscraper.

One of the most famous skyscrapers is the Empire State Building in New York City. At 1,250 feet (381 m) high (before the addition of its television tower), it was the world's tallest building for 41 years.

Getting Around—Fast

The elevators in the Burj Khalifa are the fastest in the world. They travel at 59 feet (18 m) per second. The elevators need to be fast because the building has more than 160 **inhabitable** storeys.

Word Watch

inhabitable able to be lived in

Web Watch ▼

www.skyscraper.org

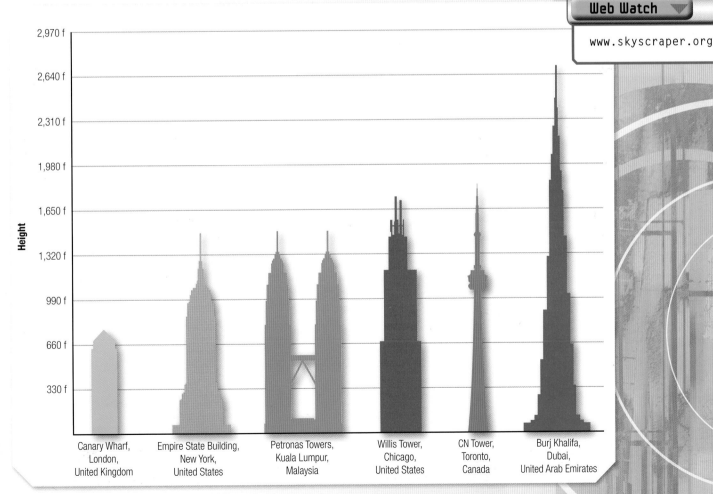

▲ The Burj Khalifa is far taller than other famous skyscrapers, and it is 2.1 times taller than the Empire State Building.

How Long Does It Take for the London Eye to Complete One Revolution?

The London Eye is a giant Ferris wheel in England that takes about 30 minutes to complete a revolution. It is 443 feet (135 m) tall. On a clear day, from the top, you can see up to 25 miles (40 km) away.

Celebrating a New Millennium

The London Eye was built to celebrate the arrival of the new **millennium** and opened in 1999. It was originally called the Millennium Wheel. The link between the wheel and the millennium is that the turning of the wheel represents the passing of time. The idea for the wheel came from a pair of architects, David Marks and Julia Barfield. When designing the wheel, they sought the advice of several other designers.

Building the London Eye

Once the design was final, the construction of the London Eye took just over a year. Sections were constructed and then transported up the River Thames, assembled and raised into position. The wheel was officially opened by then British Prime Minister Tony Blair on December 31, 1999, but it was not open to the public until March 2000.

No Longer Tallest

When it was built in 1999, the London Eye was the world's tallest Ferris wheel. Since then, it has been **surpassed** by the Star of Nanchang in China (525 feet; 160 m) and the Singapore Flyer in Singapore (541 feet; 165 m).

▲ The London Eye is located on the South Bank of the River Thames in London.

Word Watch

millennium period of 1,000 years
surpassed overtaken

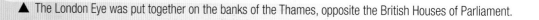

▲ The London Eye was put together on the banks of the Thames, opposite the British Houses of Parliament.

The Structure of the London Eye

The London Eye has 32 capsules, representing the 32 **boroughs** that make up Greater London. Each capsule weighs 11 tons (10 t) and holds 25 people. This means 800 people can ride on the Eye at once.

The London Eye moves because it has a spindle and hub. The spindle holds the wheel structure, while the hub rotates the wheel around the spindle. Supporting the hub and spindle are two 197-foot (60-m) high columns called the A-frame.

The **circumference** of the wheel is 1,391 feet (424 m).

The hub rotates the wheel.

Together, the wheel and capsules weigh 2,315 tons (2,100 t).

The capsules have circular mounting rings that are fixed to the outside of the main rim. This gives them a 360-degree view from the top of the wheel.

The 75-foot (23-m) tall spindle holds the wheel structure. Six huge cables secure the rear of the spindle to an underground anchor.

The A-frame supports the hub and spindle. The foundation of the A-frame required 2,426 tons (2,200 t) of concrete and 44 concrete piles. Each of the concrete piles is 108 feet (33 m) deep.

▲ Most Ferris wheels are supported on both sides, but the London Eye is only supported on one side.

Nonstop Ride

The London Eye travels 10.24 inches (26 cm) per second, which is less than 0.6 miles (1 km) per hour. At this speed, the Eye does not have to stop to let passengers on or off. They simply step on while it is moving. The Eye is stopped, however, to let on disabled and elderly people.

Word Watch

boroughs divisions of a town or area

circumference total distance around the outside of a circular area

Web Watch

www.londoneye.com

Index